DO YOU KNOW WHERE THE ENGLISH ALPHABET COMES FROM?

INTRODUCTION

Do You Know Where The English Alphabet Comes From?

As a language, English is a difficult language to learn, as there are many conventions to understand. Modern English comprises 26 letters, and their combination makes up the words and phrases so you can understand what people say. But where did the letters of the alphabet come from? Who came up with all the letters? The English alphabet has a long and complicated history, and we're going to learn the background of each letter.

OPQRSTUVWXYZ

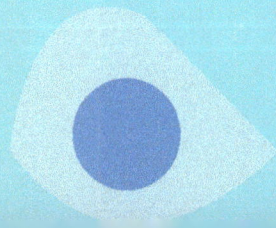

ABCD
EFGH
IJKL
MNOP
QRST
UVWX
YZ

ABCD
EFGH
IJKL
MNOP
QRST
UVWX
YZ

ABCD
EFGH
IJKL
MNOP
QRST
UVWX
YZ

ABCD
EFGH
IJKL
MNOP
QRST
UVWX
YZ

ABCD
EFGH
IJKL
MNOP
QRST
UVWX
YZ

ABCD
EFGH
IJKL
MNOP
QRST
UVWX
YZ

ABCD
EFGH
IJKL
MNOP
QRST
UVWX
YZ

ABCD
EFGH
IJKL
MNOP
QRST
UVWX
YZ

ISBN 978-1-914926-60-0

www.markosia.com

ina Beijerstam

2020

Text by Bernadine Racoma

BOOK NAVIGATOR

TABLE OF CONTENTS

A B C D E F G H I J K L M N

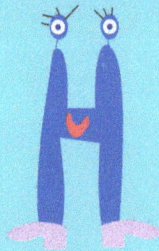

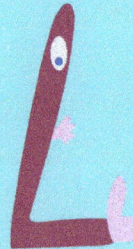

LETTERS **A** to **M**

LETTER A

A a

Linguists found that the letter A was from the Egyptian hieroglyphics, which used to represent the head of an ox with horns or antlers in an inverted teardrop form. The shape was fitting because the letter represents aleph or ox. The Greeks called it alpha, while the Romans used it as the vowel

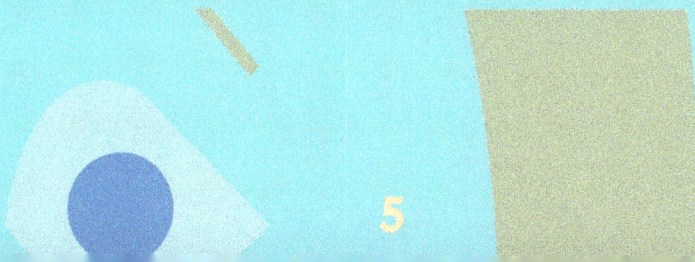

LETTER B

B b

The letter B is from Beth or the house. It was borrowed from the Egyptian hieroglyphics that was a symbol of a reed house, although the sound is more of an H. The Greeks used it to represent beta (B) while the Romans called it B.

LETTER C

C c c

This letter used to represent Gimel (camel), which used to be drawn as something that resembles a boomerang, came from the Phoenicians. In Greek, it was called gamma. On the other hand, the Etruscans used it for their K sound. The Romans, who gave it the present-day crescent shape, called it C.

LETTER D

Dd

In Egyptian hieroglyph, the letter D was the symbol for the door,

which the Semites used as the representation of Daleth.

For the Greeks, the letter D stands for Delta,

whereas it became D when the Romans used it.

LETTER E

Ee

The Greeks called this letter, Epsilon, which the Latin alphabet
gave to the English language. It came from the Egyptian
hieroglyph that looked like a man with raised hands
as if in prayer. About 3,800 years ago it represents HE, the term
for window, in the Semitic language. The Greeks gave it the "ee"
pronunciation, which became E for the Romans.

LETTER F

F F f

In the Phoenician alphabet, the letter F looked like the letter Y, with a "waw" sound. It represents a hook. Ancient Greeks named it Digamma, which the Romans shaped geometrically and named it F. "Waw" was also the origin of the letters Y, V, and U.

LETTER G

G g

In its adaptation from the Greek alphabet, the letter G appeared around 200-300 BCE, from its origin from the Egyptian hieroglyph to symbolize a throwing stick that resembles the Australian boomerang. From the letter C, the Romans added a horizontal bar and used it for the letter G.

LETTER H

H h

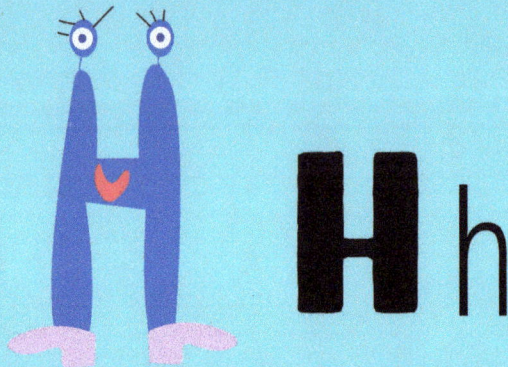

Symbolizing a fence, the letter H originated from Egyptian hieroglyphs. It had a sound created deep in the throat. The Greeks used it to represent the vowel, eta, but the Romans preferred to use it as H.

LETTER I

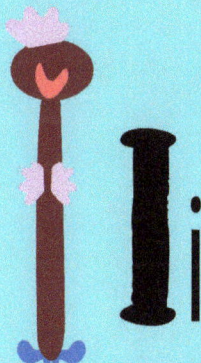

The letter I came from the Yodh letter from the Phoenician alphabet, which represented the arm and hand. The Greeks changed its form into Iota and changed it into a vertical straight line.

LETTER J

J Jj

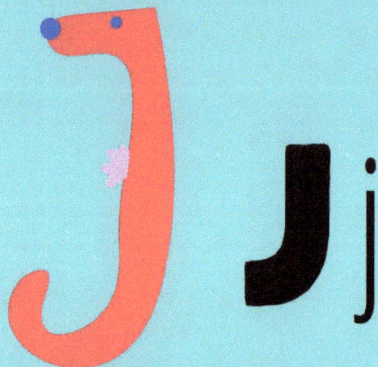

The letter J was only added to the English alphabet in the 16th century because of the influence of Spanish and French languages. It used to represent the "J" sound, and its shape, which came from the letter I, was used in the 15th century. The letter J was the last letter added to the alphabet.

LETTER K

Kk

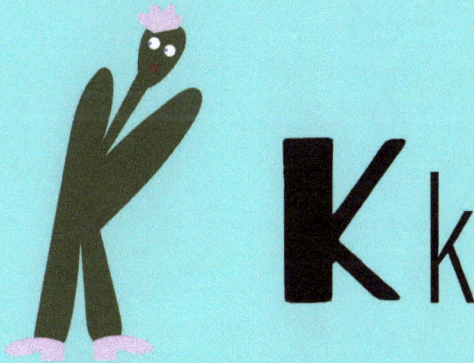

The letter K evolved from Kaf (Kaph), a Semitic letter, which came from the Egyptian hieroglyph symbolizing the palm of the hand. It represents "kappa" for the Greeks and K for the Romans.

LETTER L

Ll

In the Semitic alphabet, the letter L was upside down. The Greeks adopted the letter from the Phoenicians. It was called El, or God by the Semites. The Phoenicians reversed it, straightened the hook, and gave it the name Lamedh. It came to represent Lambda in Greek and through another variation, became the letter L for the Romans.

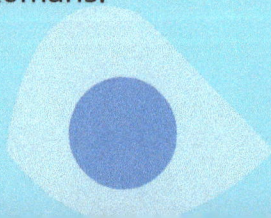

LETTER M

M m

Another letter whose origin was the Egyptian hieroglyphs, the letter M used to be a symbol for Mem or water. It used to have five peaks, which were reduced to three by the Semites in 1800 BC. The Phoenicians retained just two waves. The Greeks used the letter as the symbol for Mu, while the Romans used it to represent the letter M.

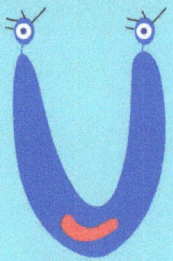

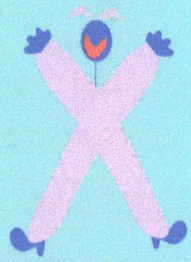
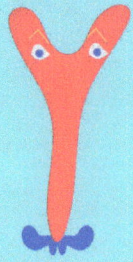

LETTERS N to Z

LETTER N

Nn

In the Egyptian hieroglyphs, the letter N represented the "eel" or "snake," (Nun), which evolved into a small ripple. From being the symbol for nu for the Greeks, it was retained by the Romans to become the letter N.

LETTER O

The letter O kept its original shape from its representation as "ayin" or eye. It was later reduced to show only the pupil. Its sound also comes from deep in the throat when it was still a consonant. The Greeks used the small O to represent omicron while the big O represented omega, which was the last letter in the Greek alphabet. The Romans used the vowel O in their alphabet.

LETTER P

P p

The letter P used to be called Pe, which is a symbol for the mouth. The Greeks called it Pi, while the Romans made modifications to it to create the letter P.

LETTER Q

In the language of the Etruscans, the letter Q was Qoph, or the symbol for wool or a monkey. Some scholars believed it symbolizes a knot, with a pronunciation that sounds like "k" expressed from the back of the mouth. In the Greek language, it symbolizes the number 90, but for the Romans and the Etruscans, it was Q.

LETTER R

R r

The letter R used to be called by the Semites and Phoenicians as Resh, or the head, became the letter rho for the Greeks and the letter R for the Romans by adding another line to differentiate it from the letter P.

LETTER S

S s s

The letter S used to be called Shin (tooth), which was written like a bow or a horizontal wave. The Greeks turned it sideways and used it as their representation of sigma. From its angular version, the Romans made the letter rounded and used it as S.

LETTER T

T t

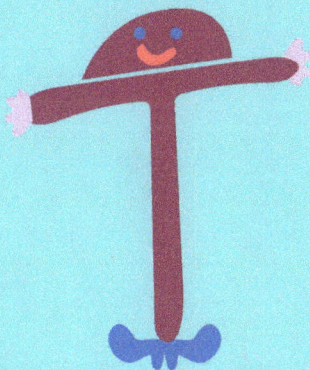

In the Phoenician, Etruscan, Greek, and Latin alphabets, the letter T consistently retained its shape and sound. From being the symbol for Taw (mark), the Greeks used it as Tau, and the Romans kept it as the letter T.

LETTER U

In 1000 BC, the present-day letter U looked like a "Y." It used to mean peg, which the Greeks used as the symbol for upsilon and the letter U for the Romans.

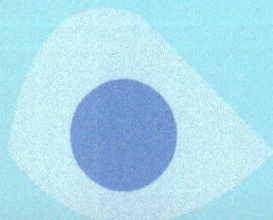

LETTER V

V V v

The letter V was used interchangeably by the Romans with the letter U. Around 1400 BC, the distinction was made permanent.

LETTER W

W w

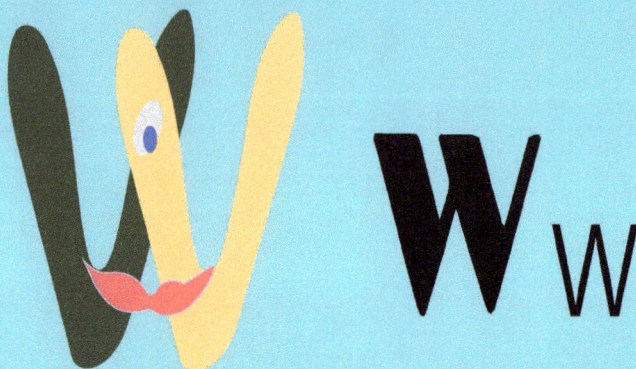

Another addition to the modern English alphabet was the letter W, which developed from the VV digraph in the 14th century. The process of creating a separate letter took three centuries to finish. In the Middle Ages, it was written as "uu" that created a V sound. Letter W first appeared in print around the 1700s.

LETTER X

X x

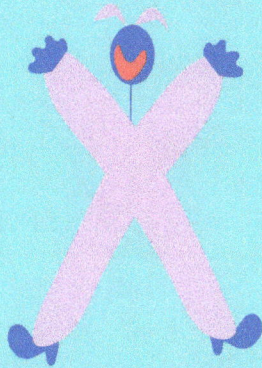

The origin of samekh (fish) is uncertain. It has strong similarities to the djed pillars of ancient Egypt. But some scholars believe it was originally from the Greeks and passed on to the Romans. The Greeks used it to represent the sound "ksi" or "xi" (chi), which was simplified into X. The Romans only retained the letter X variation.

LETTER Y

Y y

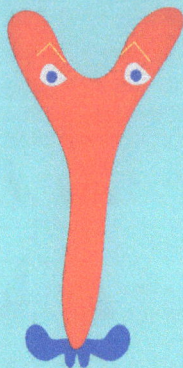

The letter Y came from the variations of the Waw, a Phoenician
letter. The Romans added the letter only around 100 AD.

LETTER Z

Z z

The letter, used to be called Zayin, may have meant an ax or sword. The Greeks made some changes to it in 800 BC and used it to represent Zeta, which was adopted by the Romans to represent the letter Z, which ends their version of the alphabet.

A, B, C, D, E, F, G, H, I,

Q, R, S, T, U and V, W,

NOW, I KNOW MY ABC's.

J, K, L, M, N, O, P

X, Y and Z

NEXT TIME WON'T YOU

SING WITH ME?

THANKS

NOW YOU KNOW HOW THE LETTERS OF THE ENGLISH ALPHABET CAME ABOUT

www.ingramcontent.com/pod-product-compliance
Lightning Source LLC
Chambersburg PA
CBHW041434040426
42452CB00020B/2970